Body Compost

& other ghost poems

Éloïse Armary

All rights reserved
© Éloïse Armary 2023

The rights of Éloïse Armary to be identified as the author of this work have been asserted by her in accordance with Section 77 of the Copyright, Designs and Patent Act 1988.

Portrait photography by Alice Pierre
Tree photography by Éloïse Armary

ISBN: 978-1-7393172-2-5

Ebook ISBN: 978-1-7393172-3-2

First edition, October 2023

"After a rain mushrooms appear on the surface of the earth as if from nowhere. Many come from a sometimes vast underground fungus that remains invisible and largely unknown."

Rebecca Solnit

"Ghosts are a lot harder to see. But when you suddenly move from a lighted room to a dark one, you can't see for a second, and that's when the dust bunnies come out."

Tatsuo Kusakabe

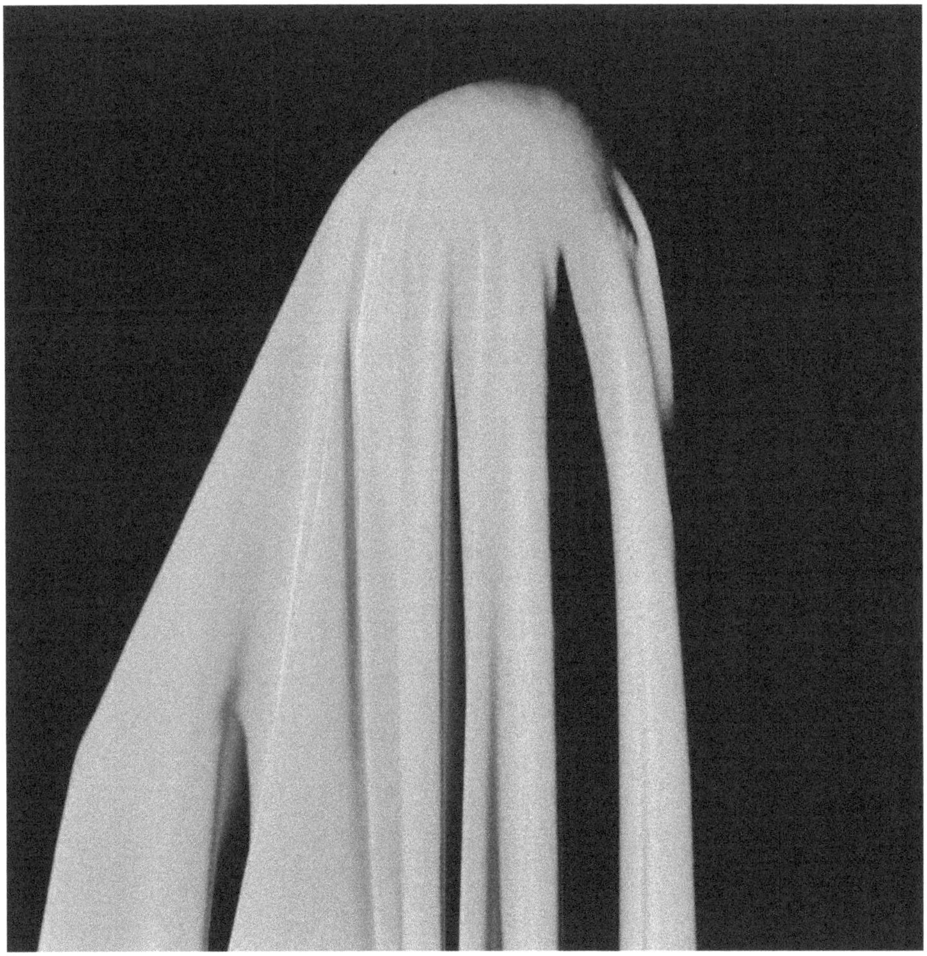

Toutes les maisons sont hantées
by dead people and children who grew into serious adults.

I look under the bed and there you are, with the dust bunnies.
There are broken balls and a tissue with undried tears
from when you lost a friend.

We are all haunted bodies living in haunted houses

and we walk into the future, still terrified of the past.
I smell the same roses as grandma, when she landed North of the
sea; *mais il n'y a pas de marché pour acheter des kilos d'épices.*

When I cook, I try to find the spices that melted under my *mamie*'s
tongue, *je sais que ma mère a tenté la même chose avec sa
grand-mère.*

We are all flavoured by phantoms; yes,
nous sommes toutes hantées par les langues de nos ancêtres.

Bottle the sewing room smell
made of the burning machine when you sewed curtains.
Feel all the threads in between your fingers,
when you inhale that cloth that I picked out for you,
a thousand miles away.

Bottle the bed linen smell,
fresh from drying in the wind in between the oaks,
warm from the tumble dryer in the rainy winter.
Do you remember when you tied my shoelaces in the morning?
I was sitting on the machine and was giggling from the vibrations.

Bottle the kitchen smell,
a mix of onions, garlic and turmeric. (*onion / ail / curcuma*)
That brought me somewhere else, to when you discovered ginger.

We're in between your heritage and our home,
the one we made in the middle of four white walls.
I baked bunches of chocolate cakes
and chocolate chip cookies,
in all the kitchens we lived in.

I don't see you sew anymore.
Tu n'achètes plus de chocolat à cuisiner.
We no longer dry the bed sheets outside.

Still,
always, always, always
your soul smells of lavender.

Why didn't you take the apartment?
You give me the keys while you park the car.
I climb up the stairs and the neighbours take me for you.

Boxes and boxes to pack,
the *secrétaire* that haunts you and creeps on me at night.
I stepped foot in here three times,
I know these walls held you.

We take a break and make some tea.
I ask, *why didn't you take the apartment*, and you say,
because these walls crushed me.
Now we're priced out of Paris and you moved out four times since.

I wonder, what if you took the apartment?
It was his apology from the country after persecution.
The cement is still mixed with yellow threads,
yet you could have healed the ghosts in the floor cracks,
hitting Tibetan bowls and vibrating your womb.

You fill up the car boot with boxes and the *secrétaire*. You
leave the keys behind. You don't tell me
what your mind holds but I understand
it weighs too much. You try to unload
the sickening taste of the past
with the ghosts in the floor cracks.

You say,
I had to say yes to something else, see what the future holds.
We ponder in between two sips.

I hear in the silence:
No more yellow threads, no more stars.
No more, no more, no more.

I hold my grandmother's porcelain vase that has been sitting on the
living room shelf. I hold my breath
when dusting it for upcoming visitors.
I bring the vase everywhere I go,
to see it under the same light
as life in the streets and coffee with my friends.
I wrap it in delicate paper, but I can hear it
breaking in my backpack with every step I make;
all I can do is hold the broken pieces in my pocket.

I shed tears for a lover I have never met. I grieve the ancestors
I have never seen the faces of,
I take their pain in,
a language I decipher by learning how to read my own.
I talk to a version of myself I have never become,

I speak to absence.

I imagine its presence in my life to create a room for it to rest.
I hold the child I used to be, the child I want to have;

all I can do is sing to ghosts.

Your bedroom doesn't exist but every night, I turn the light off.
after Will Harris

In another life, I have
tucked you in at night
watched you take your first steps
shown you through the school gangs
got heartbroken when you snuck away to smoke pot
extended my heart to keep yours unshattered
worried about you leaving me at any second
packed your suitcase when you left for uni
tried to leave you a handwritten note
couldn't find the right words because
                I am not supposed to say I love you
crushed the paper in my hand
snuck your soft toy in between your sweaters to embarrass you
                told you, I love you.

"We are all compost." Donna Haraway

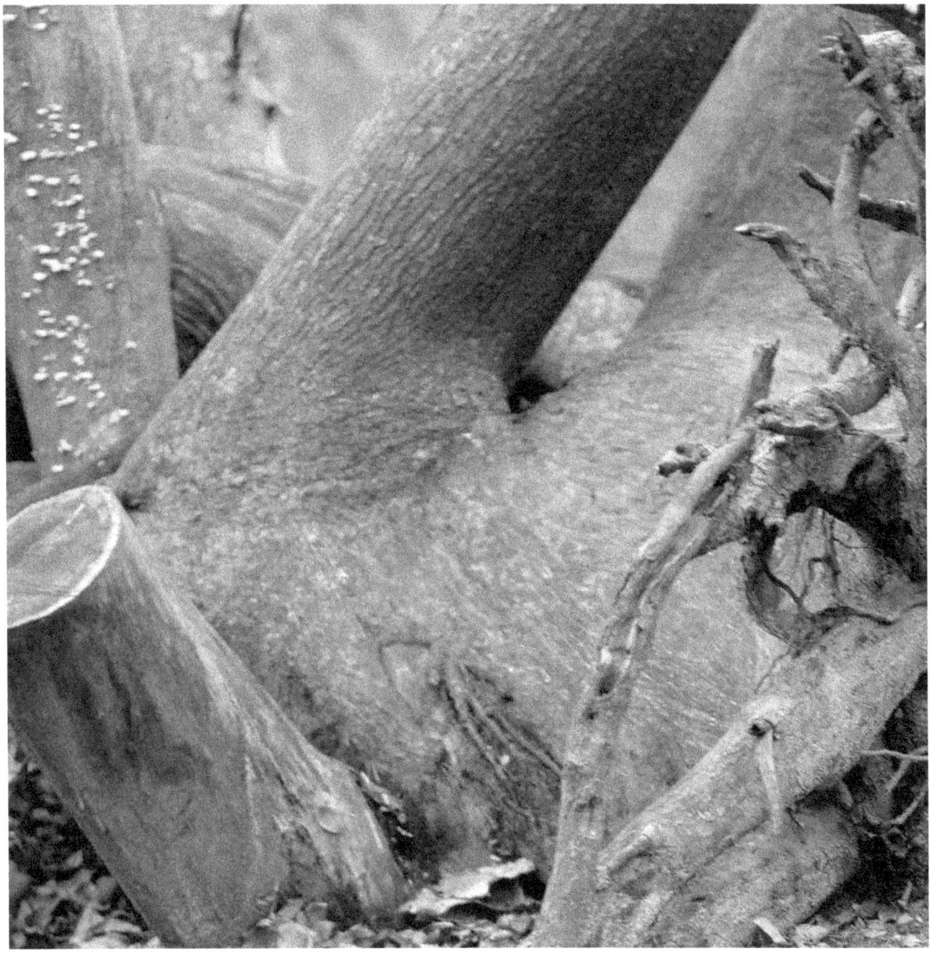

The first time I met you, I wondered how I was going to lose you. It was as easy as sharing our names, smiles and biscuits. I knew we would say we won't be strangers but become it anyway. Loving someone is preparing to hurt.

We tell ourselves we will be together forever, despite graduating, despite moving out, despite falling in love, despite depression, despite despite despite, and I believe you. Every time,
I believe you.

Every time, I find myself alone one evening, wondering how you slipped away. I collapse on the floor hearing the echo of our high pitch laughs and the depth of our confessions.

I want to freeze time at the peak of our relationship, when I feel that no one can be so close to me as you are, when we understand each other by blinking or reaching an arm out and everyone else can fuck right off.

You wanted to be someone else and I reminded you of your past self. You found someone who would double your cry. I did as well.

Every time I morph into another skin I find a partner who mirrors me. Your faces pile up at the back of my eyeballs,

skeletons of my past selves.

Every time I wish we would change together to become more alike, to challenge each other as to who we are but dust in the universe.

This time, I am alone in the dark room, holding my relationships at the edge of my eyelids.

Can you hear a scream beneath the wooden floor?

I wear Kohl eyeliner and long sleeves.
You'd think I was a metalhead.
Listen to true crime podcasts.
I listen to Debussy, Claire de lune.
Read Proust, A la recherche du temps perdu.
I hide my despair under my mascara.

Keep me under your skin.
Creep me under your teeth.
Humiliate me in front of your friends.
Belittle me in front of the walls.

I see them, looking at me, trying to take me in,
reaching their arm out from the oil painting.
I see it in her gaze. Acrylic glare.

You beat me, but I don't notice.

I fall under the floor,
where there is no light but in my throat.

In the basement,
I light up a candelabra and creep behind you,
flames reflect in my eyes.

You lit up the gas in me.

I should leave / pack my bags / I can cry in the shadows / the tears are unseen / I cry in silence / the owls hear everything at night / I should leave / I am so sad but I haven't learned what happiness is / I make crying part of my personality / until I cry of joy / of madness / my tears taste of salt / I think of the peace in the ocean / until atomic bombs / death everywhere to the depth of the world we have never seen / let us go back before humans / I should die / kill me / the world is angry / it screams into my ears when I try to sleep at night / I should die / I am angry / I haven't learned to scream / I clench my muscles and eat my anger until it gets stuck in my throat / my anger feels like worms / they won't make their way down my stomach / I should bury myself / in the forest until the bugs eat my skin / bring the shovel / I turn into dirt at night / I should bury myself / I cannot cope with the world / it can't cope with me / obviously / bury me / let me find release / in the pressure of the earth / I am not afraid of death.

I packed my bags and never said goodbye. I was afraid of what you wouldn't say. I came back. I stayed over and left again. You won't catch me this time. I overslept one night. When I got up for breakfast, you were gone. You drove to work and never kissed me bye. I made myself some scrambled eggs and took the bus. I went wherever; wherever you weren't.

Your silence ripped my flesh open and let me rot. Animals ate my guts and you stood there, watching me die. I made myself again from the earth filled with blood. I became part of the wolf that ate me the first time.

I rolled my suitcase and waited for the bus. We drove and I stepped off when the sun was setting. I put my bags down and started over in a new town. I was a fool but I had no choice. I left, came back and left again after that. I rolled a suitcase and Sisyphus rolled a rock, condemned to hope.

Heaviness will fade away as we get stronger. It feels harder every time I leave.

"Poetry is the way we help give name to the nameless so it can be thought. The farthest horizons of our hopes and fears are cobbled by our poems, carved from the rock experiences of our daily lives."

Audre Lorde

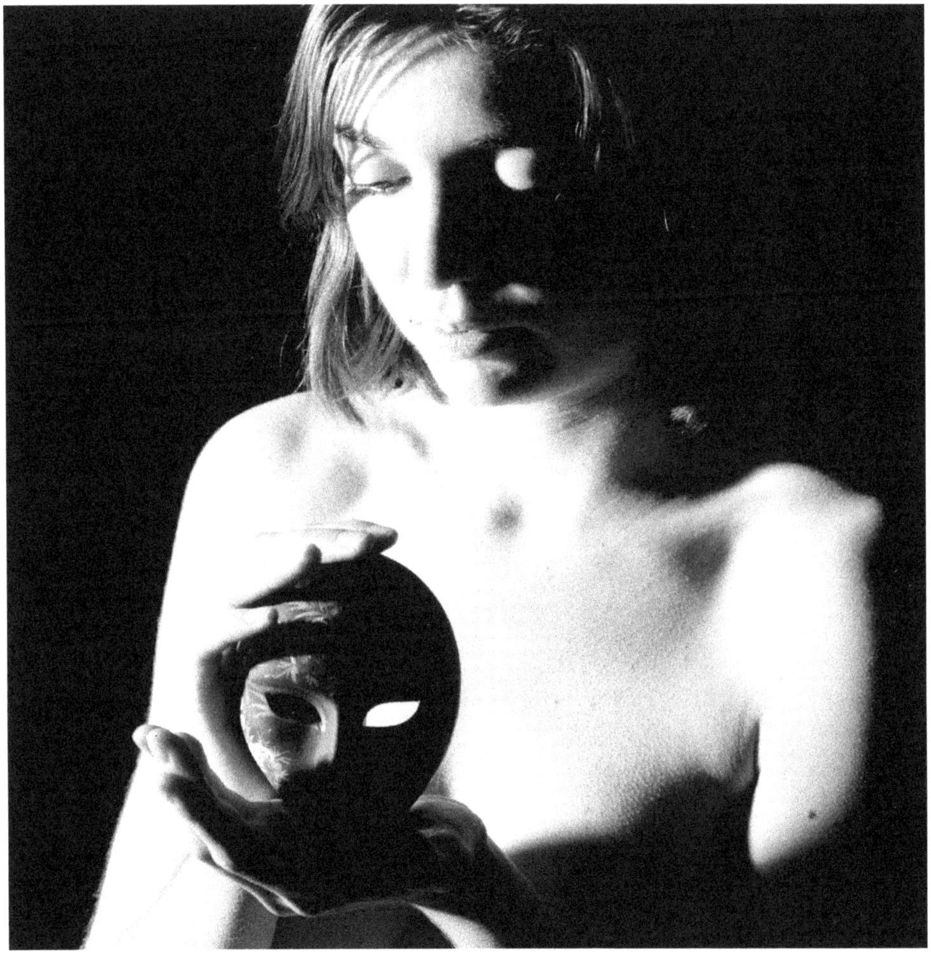

It's blurry.
I seem to be lying down on my back,
spreading my legs in the pond,
reaching for the reed at the far end.
I lay with the *nénuphar*,
finally away from deafening cars.
I roll around and stir the water,
braiding my hair in a hundred nattes.

Ma grenouille. Tickle my skin and stroke my cheeks.
I stand, starstruck, stutter in between my teeth.

Disappear under the water until you lose count.
Eyes open, I look at the *roseau*, rooted in mud.
Finally away from the blinding *phares*.

Les libellules tournent autour de nous,
singing lullabies to my ears filled with fast rushing blood.

We're back in the city.
Window licking in the mall for men and women.
I'm too mad for anyone to get me.

The water Lily already got to me.

Divinité de la mare, reed rooted in the mud.
I sink back inside the pond.

My tongue loses its grasp in your soil as it's making roots on a
further land. You didn't hold me back, you grew other seeds.

                You are sad now,

seeing so few flowers of mine.

If only you could look at me, blossoming
on the other side of the fence.

You tell me I am poorly rooted,
I don't want to nourish your garden.

It makes me want to take my branches elsewhere,
where each sprout is a gift.

                Be sad, now.

I won't turn my trunk into a willow tree because tears are the only
thing your eyes focus on.

I will nourish my blossoming flowers.

When I can't sleep I want to reach for my phone but should avoid the blue light.

when do I / stop sinking / stop thinking / who am I / without tiny pills / when I don't bleed / does seeing the world underexposed / make me see more details in the image / once in the software / once every new moon / does seeing the bright side blind you? / sun, my love, please shine on my burnt eyeballs for longer / does wearing all the colours give justice to each of them / who am I / a laugh or an aphorism / held or abandoned / who am I / who am I / without you / who am I / who am I?

I want to come under your skin
and know how your heart feels.
Hear its variations from a soft ballade to a metal concert.

I want to know if you sleep at night
and hear what keeps you awake.
Eat the food you grab to fill the empty time.

I want to hear your thoughts
on your favourite humans.
Smell the undertones in the fragrance of your life.

I want to hear your laugh,
your heartfelt chuckles.
Witness you relive your fondest memory.

I want to know you
beyond the words you tell.
Words are pieces of the story you are writing for your epitaph.

I only have the words you give me to hold onto,
knowing your ashes will be sprinkled in the sky.

I was tiny, like a pea in your hands.
I trusted you not to crush me.
You pressed your thumb against me anyway.
I couldn't escape.

I walked along with you,
hoping for you to become smaller.

You never did.

I kept up with the pace,

                                      growing larger.

I ran on the sidewalk, danced before you to make you laugh.

You smiled and I missed a heartbeat.
If I lit up this cell, I would forget that I lived in a prison.
Yet every night, I dreamt of sunflower fields.

The most difficult word to learn in French is *pardon*.

Apologise after I tell you that you hurt me.
Take your coat off after I kneel to you, tears leaving vulnerable,
naked trails down my skin.

Each word you say is a scarf you wrap around your head until your
skull suffocates.

Instead of salt water, you sugarcoat wounds with niceties;
I thought you were going to tend to the injury on my arm.

I am left alone and cannot press a cloth against it,
I pour vodka from a nearby bottle and scream into space.
High, I blink and open my eyes.

I see the laceration lies on your forearm, not mine.
Your skin is covered with fresh gashes and old scars mixed with
cotton threads, tattered clothes you covered yourself with.

I hope, one day, you will meet someone,
kneel naked in front of them, desperate to be by their side, and peel
your layers off until you are swimming in a pond of your tears.

Saying sorry is a medicine much softer than vodka bottles.

"Slowly disintegrating (relationships) are like. i miss you. i love you. i wish so many good things for you. i wish for all the love u can get. i wish i was eating chaat with u rn. i hope we never meet again."
@khlut

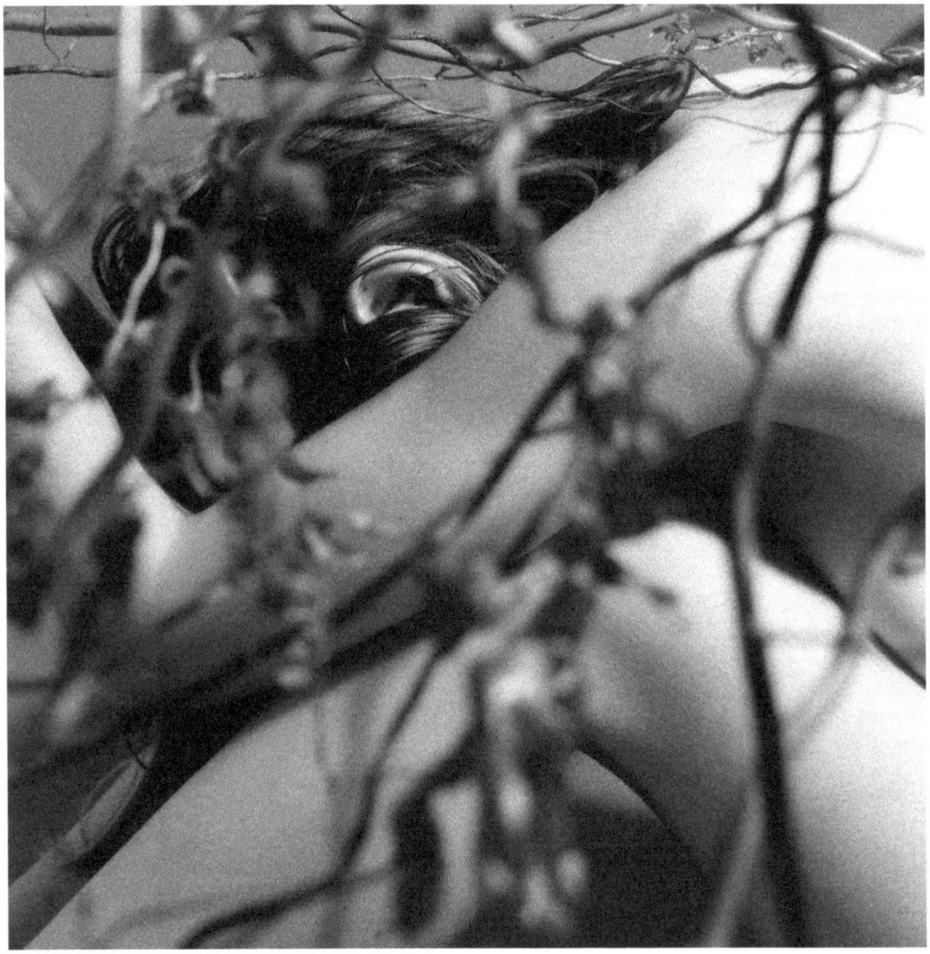

I drive by a rotten house.

I walk through the door unannounced.
You didn't want me to know there was a party.
(did you?)

We hug so tight, I choke.
You are happy to see me.
(are you strangling me with your elbows?)

I stomp my muddy boots on your white carpet.
I apologise three times about the carpet.
(i don't want you to stare at my ripped socks.)

You tell me not to worry,
you would eat on a filthy floor.
(you once taught me all the natural recipes to remove wine stains.)

You lend me a drink.

We laugh through the noise our teeth make against the glass,
you want to kiss me.
(are you scared that I will steal your girlfriend?)

I stop drinking after my stomach hurts,
I gobbled the beers too fast.
(i inhaled your perfume too deep.)

I dance with a boy. You dance with your girl.
I look at the sticky floor. You would never eat off it.

(i know I will come home alone tonight.)

it's my birthday next week
let's all go to the cinema
we'll get popcorn   and   milkshakes

remember
we went to the cinema
for my birthday
you went to the restaurant I recommended

got lost on the way
asked me for the address
texted you from my bed

had a party without me
had two parties without me
had ten parties without me

i am a ghost to you

Loulou is a body made of pink goos.

Open my past,
a collection of jams to spread on your breakfast toast.
I am an open fridge.
Come in with a spoon.
Open each lid.
Take a bit of fig jam.
Throw it over the homemade meals in Tupperware,
the oat milk carton and the two-week-old vegetables.
Cover me with a mix of orange and strawberry,
mixing the bitter and sweet taste.
I had made the blackberry jam this summer
after picking the fruits up in the forest.
Empty the whole lot in your mouth.
Spill it on your white shirt.
Close me.
Tell your sister I didn't have anything you wanted.
I will stay there, humming my tune.
Grieving my collection of jams.

Available at 18h (Paris time)?

I call
*allô**allô*
*coucou**c'est loulou*
how are you
I know

you lie I lie   in the space   between words
I whisper
I care
I love you

you hang on   stay with me
you are proud of me
we kiss in the silence

bisous
it was nice talking to you

"It's not possible to constantly hold onto crisis. You have to have the love and you have to have the magic. That's also life."
Toni Morrison

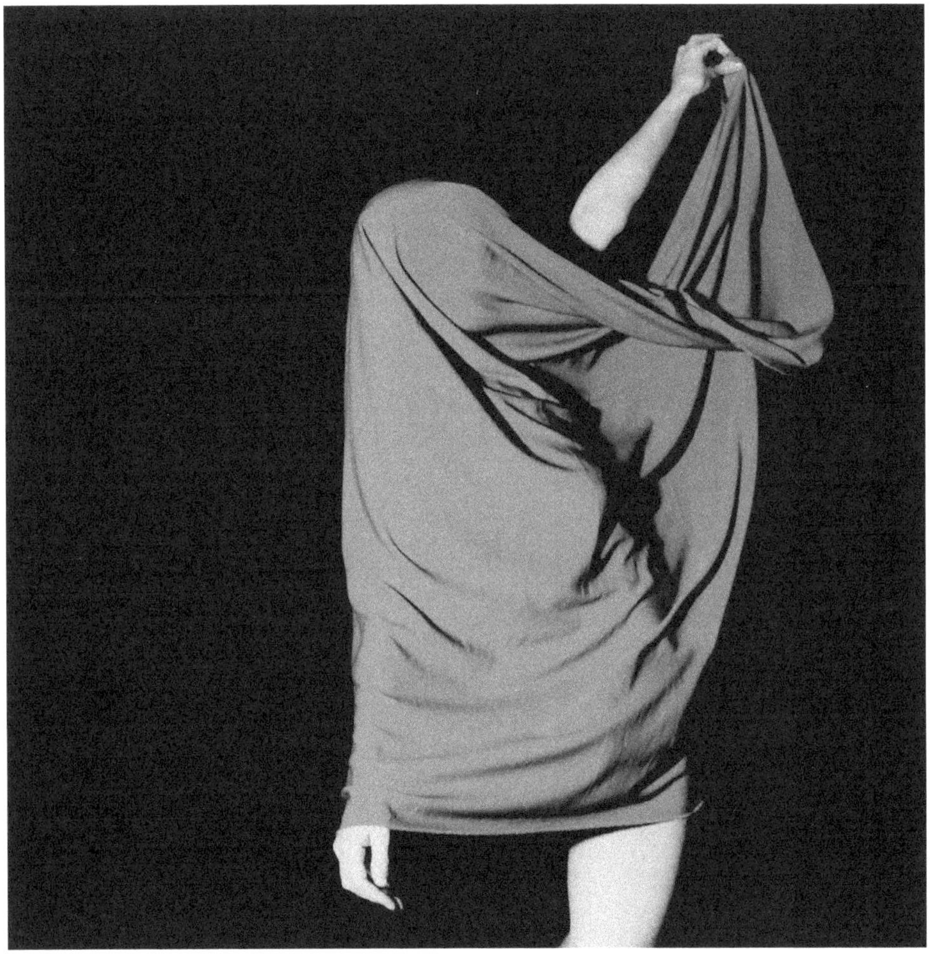

We're entering the Cyberpunk age.

A fox passes by in the city high street.
What would cities look like if all shops closed and people died?
Shops are still open and they dance to beats of death,
the *néant* never is far away; we better make it part of us.
I bite into my fish and chips in the pouring rain, the flesh is warm
and the grease sticks to my fingers even after I lick them.
I invited you to my funeral of young lady,
I don't understand why becoming family with a person I love
means that I died.
Do we preserve life or create nothingness by making scattered
dance moves in between two white pills?
I can see your eye bags darkening as dawn approaches.
You are tired of life so you decided not to sleep, partying without a
smile in city basements.
I have been thinking of it lately,
When you spoke of her and made me fall in love with someone I
will never meet.

One day you won't need to pay for four white walls, chasing away mould with bleach and vinegar; you know you should wear a mask when spraying bleach.
Would you like to grow a garden with me and read of lives that don't exist?
You eat slugs in lettuce, foxes eat garbage in overflowing bins and I understand,
wearing pink and a smile doesn't preserve me from staring into the abyss —
I share my chips with you even though you've had dinner and I've only had breakfast. I squeeze the bag of cheap ketchup out on the paper and we dip our chips in the city high street.
We stare into the darkness and watch skeletons dance under the water surface.

We made a home where time doesn't exist.

We talk about it as if the story was in our words.
We collect dreams like your grandma collects magnets.

When you don't settle, all lands are made of gold.

Music in the car, hands floating through the window,
we never turned the power on.

We closed our eyes.
We could feel the wind, the fuel and the manure,
the sunset and the dizziness in our legs from driving for so long.

We pack our bags and clean the house,
we broom the floor, wash the dishes and iron our clothes,
even the underwear.

We write the shopping list for essentials,
pot noodles and instant coffee. I already miss coffee beans.

We have breakfast next to our bags, ready to go
and stay for lunch. The news freezes and our freezer stays full,
even though we eat ice cream every day.

I make you dinner and you wrap your arms around me while the
veggies are sizzling. I spend all day looking at your cheeks,
moving mountains as you smile. I want to make you laugh over
and over just to see your craters form.

You touch my skin and turn me into a river,
I am swimming inside myself, giggling at the fish against my legs.

We move together as if Europe and America collided with each
other. Our people meet and make meals that speak louder than
languages.

We scratched all the countries from the world map.

We are the world,
but our contours feel so big, we will never touch all our edges.

After dinner, I rest my head on yours.
after Chen Chen

your chest is a blanket to rest on
— & I stroke your palm like the most delicate jewel,
I massage you from the shoulders to the bottom of your feet,
your skin is baby milk,
you are born under my fingertips,
— & I kiss all your hair
and where you have none
you hold me tight & I get you loose
my touch slips inside of you
— & I show you how much love
I have on my hands.

Can you parent the unborn?

I bring you everywhere with me.
I whisper to you all of my thoughts.
I will never let you think figuring out life was easy.
You won't have to struggle alone.

I talk you through the fears I had at eight years old.

You have a friend in me.
I stroke you and sing softly to your ears,
you relax like the cat,
leaving all the anxieties of being human
by the bedside
with your tiny slippers.

I feel calmer too,
knowing that you can breathe
deeper than I do.

"I've always wanted to have a haunted house. It's been my lifelong dream!"
Tatsuo Kusakabe

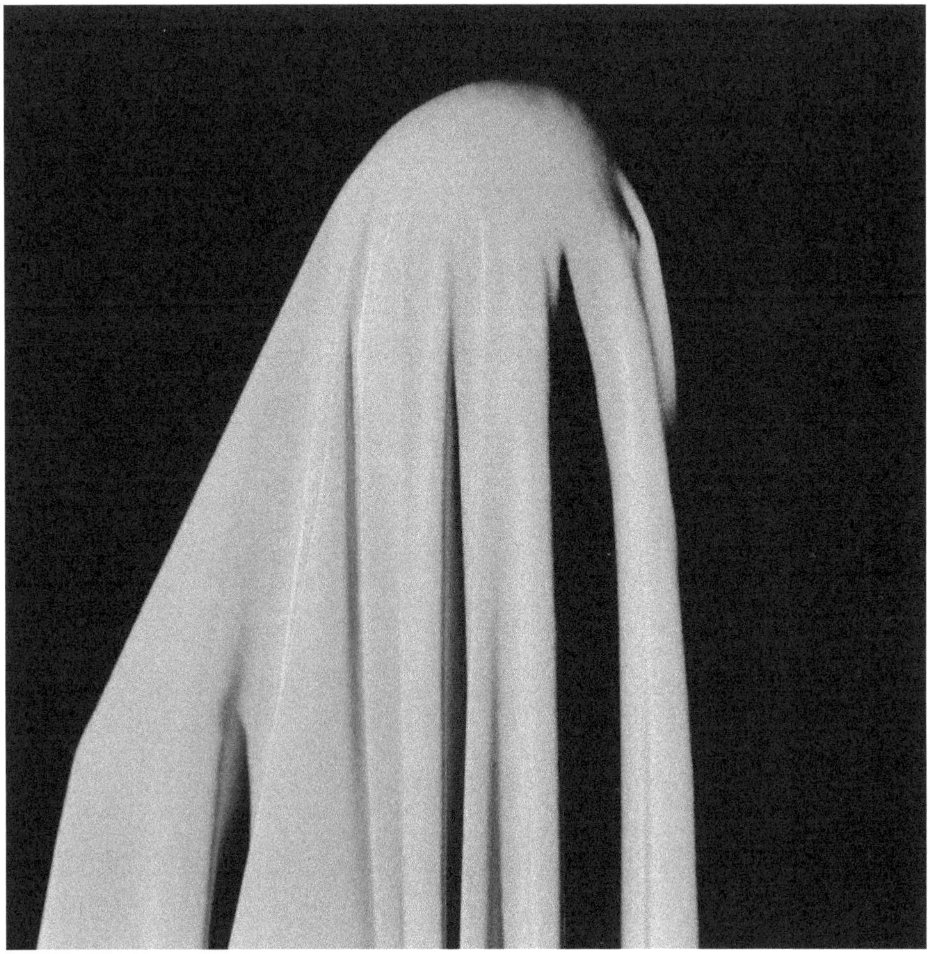

It's raining, come dance.
after Savannah Brown

(you)
when reaching for a hot coffee cup
showing your soft belly;
your hands grabbing a tray and finding

(me)
rolling over the grass
the sun's glare making me cry;
your touch softer than

(the sun)
resting in the air.
Each day feels slower now,
the world's shadows stretching more than

(the cat)
rolling over the grass
showing his soft belly;
his eyes brighter than

(you, me, the sun, the cat)

I left,
the sun was eating me
I wanted my bones to burn
I came back,
cut onions on a wooden board

my knife said: *you are worth crying for*

on the radio channel
(that I didn't turn on) journalists told
your story to the eager village

in the silence, I danced,

I saw you blink in the shadows
la pupille brillante
glittery water that makes the sea
we drove to the lake
heard only our breath,

for the first time, I opened my eyes under water

I cooked meals *(spice splash)*
we jumped into the lake *(splash splash)*
we turned the radio off *(static panic)*
I danced in silence *(socks swoosh)*

and one day,
on the ride back home,
you talked
&
I listened.

Mulch box for your body compost

Music
Body compost & other ghost songs (playlist on Spotify)
Pomme, Consolation
Lana Del Rey, Born To Die

Movies
My neighbour Totoro, Hayao Miyasaki
Aftersun, Charlotte Wells
The Braves (*Entre les vagues*), Anaïs Volpé

Books
SL Grange, Bodies and other haunted houses
Maggie Bowyer, Allergies
Savannah Brown, Closer baby closer

Non-fiction
Donna Haraway, Staying with the Trouble
Rebecca Solnit, Hope In The Dark
Tori Tsui, It's Not Just You

Online
@petrichara (Instagram)
@deadpoetsnbooks (Instagram)
How to survive the end of the world, adrienne maree brown & Autumn Brown (podcast)

Éloïse Armary (she/they) is an artivist: artist-activist. Born in Burgundy from parents of Pied-Noir and Jewish heritage, she spent her childhood in sunflower fields before moving to Paris. Growing up a flutist and saxophonist, Éloïse started writing poetry in English in Montreal when falling in love and started dabbling in photography, podcasting and filmmaking along the way. Éloïse sees beauty in the darkness and finds joy in all corners of life. They write from an ecofeminist, neurodivergent, queer and multicultural perspective. They are the co-host of Poetry To Your Ears, author of *Pink Goo* and director of *Collections Of Queer Poets*. They live in Sussex, UK with their fiancé, cat, plants and garden creatures.
Body Compost & other ghost poems is their second poetry book.

@eloisearmary
www.eloise.armary.com

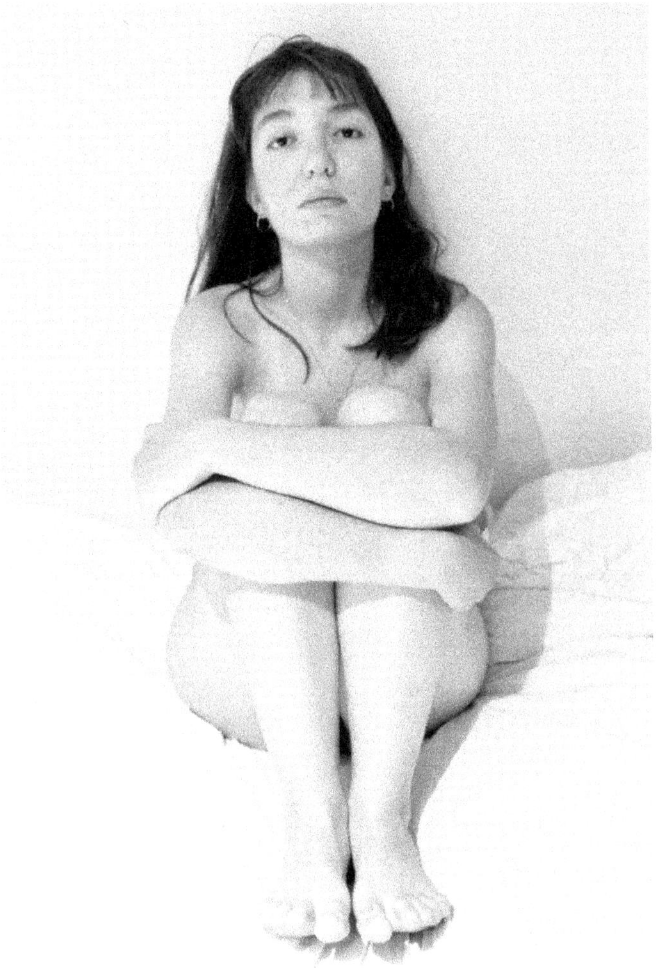

Dedicated to Tom, my roots

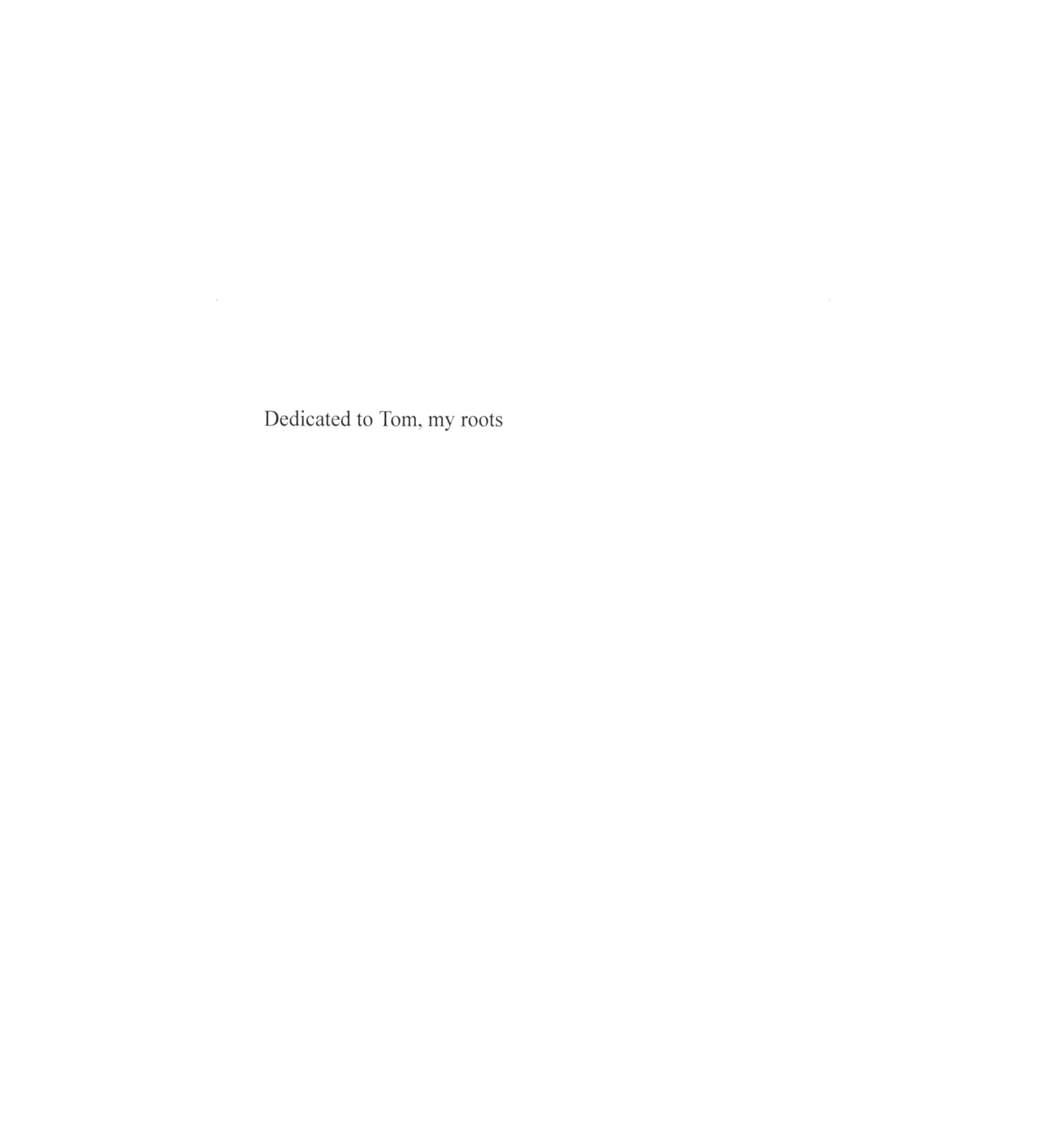

Milton Keynes UK
Ingram Content Group UK Ltd.
UKHW050829231023
431156UK00009B/80